POETIC HEALING

108 poems

SAYEH GOLD

Poetic Healing
108 poems

Sayeh Gold

Printed in the United States of America
First Printing 2021
First Edition 2021

10 9 8 7 6 5 4 3 2 1

Cover illustration by Lauren Keller

From heartbreaks to unconditional love
from fear to faith
from pain to peace
poetic healing is the journey back to myself
enjoy every wave
of this deep and vast ocean
of my heart
may it help you in your own healing
may it help you see
and recognize your divinity
may you absorb every poem
like a sip of your favorite tea
may you be loved
and may you be happy

Love,
Sayeh.

CONTENTS

LOVE, LUST & LOSS

my first love was my father
I saved his life when I was three
since then I have tried to save all men
who pretended to love me

and now
I can hear the city crying
I can hear my ego yelling
I can hear my father dying
but layer by layer
I can hear my heart healing

-first love

you are a rock on the outside
and a soft flower on the inside
your smile sings to me when it shines
and your love has saved me many times
the beat of your heart is on repeat
and your touch has never failed me
your courage is yet unknown to you
but it does reflect on me
and every time I am with you
I feel safe to be me
when you leave the world ends
my sorrows remind me of your absence
I count the days and pray
until I can hold your heart again
countless times I have pushed you away
the doubts and the fears of my heart breaking once
more
terrifies me more than all the evil in the world
because with your love I can survive everything
because with your love I am invincible

-god sent

summer love
with nobody to love
it's summer love
and I have nobody

I miss the heat
and I miss your love
I miss your heart
and I miss your hug
I miss your touch
and the sun so much

summer love
with nobody to love
it's summer love
and I have nobody

nobody to love
nobody to kiss
I have nobody to hug
and I'm nobody's bliss

-summer love

no one speaks in poetry
no one delivers their love authentically
they are afraid of love
how did it become such a thing

they share their beds and intimacy
their bodies and their sweat
they blend like a cactus and a flower
and they don't mind bleeding to death
until their heart is dry
until their soul dies

-modern love

when your faith is back
can you hold on tight
can you promise you won't let me go
one more time

when the storm is over
and the flowers bloom
your heart will beat again
the seeds of your love will grow

and when you're done
hating yourself
maybe you can
love me again

-faith

every petal you tore
from every flower we shared
from all the thousands of kisses
you shamelessly stole from my lips
and the countless lies
my poor mind didn't buy
there's one thing you couldn't be
the heart inside of me
so no matter how bad you were to me
I forgive you for hating me

-love thief

I wish we could've all grown apart peacefully
I wish ego wasn't such a big part of me
I wish so many things went differently
that our love was what it used to be
people I considered family
left a big scar in me
they must've got it wrong
this passion and fire in me

-old friends

I will die a million times
until love conquers all
once and for all

-servant of love

love doesn't make us blind
love gives us courage
love gives us strength
and shame on everyone
who mistreated your heart
forgive them
forgive yourself
you have learned
but most importantly
you have loved
fearlessly

-fearless

the ocean is not a safe place for shallow souls
so when he said *I want to get to know your heart*
I kindly replied *I hope you know how to swim*

-ocean heart

I wish I was disgusted by the sight of you
after the things you did
but you were as beautiful as ever
it was hard to admit
considering the hate I carry for you
the veil of your face
hid the ugliness of your heart
the sun reflecting on your smile
made my soul blind
I never got a chance to throw a chair at your face
and all the anger I accumulated
you deserved it and more

-bitterness

my heart breaks so my soul can heal

-sacrifice

the coldness of your heart
penetrated my being
like your penis penetrated my soul
and fucked all the senses out of me

I walked in shame with integrity
a pure and devastating emotional hangover
until you were taken away from me
I will consume you over and over

I know the devil is behind you
but he is making you look so good
I'll let you dry me out
until I have no reason to walk away anymore
and simply drink your fraudulent love

I'll betray anything
just so I can be with you
I await your attention
like a drunk waits for his favorite bar to open

-lust

I love the energy you channel in me
you make me feel alive honey
play channel orange and make love to me
make my skin glow like golden hour baby

-love vessel

I can feel you get closer to me
I talk to you like you were already here
where are you now
are you happy
are you also looking for me
I'm here and I'm ready

-divine love

your love is overwhelming
effortless and genuine
I am amazed by the dedication you have
to take care of me
you bring me tears of joy daily
nothing compares to the sincerity of your heart
you make me happy with admirable ease
your love is fluid and simple
my heart feels safe my heart feels home
you are like a perfect wave in the ocean
a blissful sunset
a divine flower
a flawless full moon

-love letter

my heart is my weapon and I'm not afraid to use it

-love warrior

after every heartbreak
my love grows
and for my heart to heal
it needs some holes

-growth

if my heart could talk
it would tell you how much it loves you
if my hand could talk
it would tell you how much it wants to touch you
if my soul could speak
it would tell you how much I miss you

-my whole being

I am grateful for all the pain because it was the only way to you

thank you for being a mirror of my love
a reflection I haven't seen often maybe never
you hold a special place in my heart forever

-to a real friend

I have to enjoy the sun without you
or should we face winter together
can we meet in the middle of spring
and create our own summer
build a strong foundation
no fall

the seasons aren't the same without you
flowers don't look the same
the sunlight hurts
the full moon
reminds me how empty
I am without you

-seasons change

I'm afraid to fall asleep
I can't tolerate your absence
in the middle of the night
all I do is write about you
and since you can't save me
I'm hoping at least my poetry
will save me from the agony
from the pain of you leaving me
and since I can't have you next to me
I don't see the point of reality
induce me into eternal sleep
may your touch be
all that can awaken me

-you're my remedy

you haven't been so present lately for me for us
I know sometimes you have those periods
where you retract
I know you are still learning to cope with your emotions
I learned that forcing it out of you
won't do anything helpful
all I can do is be here and be patient
I feel powerless at times
because I have no clue how you feel
my whole life people used and abused me
now I listen to their problems every day
help them heal from traumas that I often relate
in between the two
I am working hard on not putting you in the same boat as anyone
trying not to take personal your detachment
I am running low on patience
due to my past and not specifically you
I am torn between being the one to reach out
even when you don't
or to wait sometimes that you do
so it leaves space for you to open up
I don't know which is the best
I have been conditioned to toxic ways for so long
and just learning now all about unconditional love
so I still struggle with where is the limit with you

I offer you the space to be happy
but if you can't choose happiness for yourself
there is not much I can do
so I pray god helps you in ways that I can't
I just hope you're okay
goodnight

-late night text

qué hermosa es la luz
pero para qué mirar la luz si no tengo a nadie conmigo
no tener a nadie con quien compartir la luz
hace que mi alma pierda todos sus sentidos
la luz no tiene ningún propósito
si no hay nadie con quien compartirla
así que dime amor
por qué molestarse en buscarla
si no estás aquí a mi lado

how beautiful is the light
but why look at the light if I have no one with me
have no one to share the light with
makes my soul lose all its senses
the light has no purpose
if there is no one to share it with
so tell me love
why bother looking for it
if you are not here by my side

-la luz

I spend my days waiting
waiting to think
so I can think about you
I find pleasure in music again
and all the songs that
left a bitter taste in my heart
you turned them into love again
I wake up feeling joy again
knowing love again
and I don't have enough of a lifetime
to thank you for your loving heart

-passion

the sun danced at your arrival
the moon celebrated us
the flowers bloomed
and the water was breathing

-sacred union

love is not a matter of time
love is a matter of courage and detachment
of worthiness and faith
it's not a matter of logic or common sense
love doesn't make sense
there is nothing rational about love

so many firsts we explored together
my experience with you is permanently on my body
I know your inner child is crying
and waiting to be loved properly
but if I stayed and didn't choose me
this would've ended badly
so I let go of all my love for you and passed it to god
for it is not my destiny to come in the way of
your journey

-I am no one's savior

I am not mad at you nor do I resent you
I pray for you
and I pray that god keeps showing up in your life
I know all of this was divine
no matter how difficult it was
I pray that you find the courage
to go within those wounds
and the root of it all
knowing you are loved and supported by your spirits
you are an amazing human and you deserve to heal
and be the best version of yourself
you have lots of love to give
but it's time for you to show up for yourself

-love yourself then you can love me

I had a lifetime with you in a matter of days
your love came in like a flashing light
it all appeared to be like a dream
when I woke up the next day
and as I ascend
my lessons are shorter
but the heartbreaks are stronger
every minute I spent with you
I knew I was just a moment away
from losing you

-blink of an eye

being in love
and not being in love
are the only states I know
and only dimensions I grow

-to be or not be

SELF

they told me I wasn't who I am
they told me don't feel the way you do
they told me I was special
but to keep it to myself
they said don't be yourself
but be yourself around me
I can use someone like you
I love you I hate you so much
and since my body was such a shame
I made a living out of it
they lay eyes on me
like they own me
the gods and spirits did not create me
for your incestuous mind
no magic no past
don't you see everything you stole
finds its way back home

-woman

they will drink my blood when my flesh is rotten
long gone in the ruins of my old town
they will read my soul as they know it so well
they will joyfully cheer to my existence after death has taken me
they will celebrate me long after I perished
they will lie and tell my story as if they know anything about me
I sacrificed my heart so those with poor judgment
can find a sense to their meaningless life
and those who didn't believe in me
are now drinking the outcome of my suffering
I have arisen in a time where my evolution was nothing but a comedy
oh they have fallen asleep for so long
when they finally awaken
I was gone in the ruins of my old town

-montreal

I am not a healer
just a sinner
who found meditation
and poetry

-redemption

I write from the darkest place
where the wounds are invisible to the eye
my body knew no tragedy
all the chaos lives in me
they might think I have no credibility
but I've felt more than anyone
more than anybody
I understand pain
and there's enough space in my heart
to handle all the rain

-scorpio moon

young lost and confused
I vowed to leave the very place
that was holding the secret
the meaning of my existence
the door
the portal of every existential question I had
it was right there in front of my blind eyes
wide open for me to freely take the leap of faith
everyone who crossed that gate has a different story
and even myself I have crossed it more than once
and each time it was a different tale
I was familiar with the outside noise
the music in bars
friends yelling and laughing
the sound of the city and cars drifting
neighbors stomping
but I have never heard something
as loud as the silence
the silence of my demons
tearing my organs one by one
an empty orchestra
a silent concert
where I was the lead singer
and the only spectator

-vipassana

he is on the death row of my life
I resent him for choosing his demons over his light
he probably wishes to be gone
but as I honor our mission
his sentence is to remain alive

-karma

there is just too much history
but I found a safe space for my sins in poetry
there's a story behind the light
a light that didn't come for free

if I stop making mistakes
then how would I write poetry
I will have nothing to write about
I will have no stories to share

-life imitates art

you are beautiful strong and loving
you are sensitive
caring and innocent
you were brought here for a very special mission
a love mission
you were chosen
don't let this dark path fool you
you will have access to a light
your light
turn your awareness to that light and find me
I will always look after you
I am always there
and it hurts me more than it hurts you
to know the suffering that I will put you through
but let me tell you how beautiful you still are
stronger than you ever were
as loving as you always wanted to be
love is your driven force and it is an honor to be me
to have never given up on love is your power
I love you
I love me
may we all be happy
and may we all be free

-inner child

I sacrifice my happiness
so I can write poetry
so I can have a story to share
so the sad of this world
can read my words
and feel less lonely
I sacrifice it all
so one heart can be happy
so one story can end greatly
so one life can be lived fully
while I am unhappy
broken and in misery
I love to see happiness
in others more than in me

-self-sacrifice

poems are more than assembled words
poetry is a feeling
it's that feeling of overwhelming joy
when you sit in the sun and for a moment
you truly feel peace and silence
and it's like your chest opens up to the world
you see clear
you see god
you understand the mission you're on
the energy is pulling out of my crown
and my soul wants to come out of my body
my organs are sitting in fire
my throat wants to cry
my eyes want to close
a feeling of bliss
a poem is a feeling of bliss

-bliss

I did everything while crying
I did everything while fighting
I did everything while healing
I did it all while someone was breaking my heart

all the broken pieces I worked putting together
together while I was loving

I loved while I was hating
I loved while I was cheating
I loved while I was sinning
I loved everything and everyone
while I despise
while I despised it all

-polarities

I'm cleansing from my demons
and might have lost the love of my life
the devil looks so good in others
but in me it looks hideous
there is an odd satisfaction
when the storm of my darkness passes by
there is some peace and calm
and sometimes hope
from here maybe I can do better

-demons

les éclairs chantent ma rage
pendant que je pleure dans la pluie
une mélodie accompagnée du ciel et de l'orage

mes larmes ne font qu'un avec les gouttes d'eau
pendant que mon coeur fais son deuil dans l'ombre de
ma joie

-l'orage

in the midst of all this
I still feel pure bliss
my bliss is not defined by you
my bliss is like air
it is there whether you like it or not
like the air you can't live without it
and always took it for granted

-contentment

she makes men read her poetry
she pretends they look like
what she would want them to be
they read her soft words of love
as she travels in her imaginary world

-fantasy

the sky is still blue
the sun is still shining
there might be a storm in my head
but I'm still worth living

-storms

love is art and just like an artist without a muse
I am useless without my heart

the work I do will not show fruit
until I am long gone
this world is both wild and quiet
abundant and musty
it's a strange place
as if the unconditional love of mother earth
was so overwhelming
we found a way to sabotage it
it's too much greatness
let's bring chaos
why you ask
let me know when you know

I don't know how such darkness
can bring such magic
everywhere I go a room lights up
some hearts start singing
flowers start growing
I bring joy and music
freedom and magic
yet I feel dead inside
and I have been for a while
this light is in service of others
because quite frankly
this light no longer has an effect on me
I am simply a transporter of this light
a messenger of love
my only purpose is to bring a smile
but this heart of mine
is no longer alive

-magic

I still find it fascinating
to be who I am when I am not myself
I learn a lot from who I am not

-ego

I was never dumb
and I was never blind
I was wide awake
the whole fucking time

sometimes I would put myself in situations
where I knew I would get hurt
that way I was able to manage my pain
but I wasn't prepared for the coldness of this world
I was not meant for winters or players
I wasn't meant for clubs and fast money

-soul contract

do you know how many times I had to fake a smile
so no one would know how sad I was
you wouldn't know because it's very similar to my real smile

-mask on

wouldn't it be nice if all our muses were just
flowers flourishing eternally
if our muse was the sun rising
every morning
no matter the season
but then where is the depth
my favorite muses are all the heartbreaks
every moment I chose pain over love
I can write about my misery every day

-misery is poetry

every layer of sorrow I healed
is wrapped around my heart
like a victory belt

it gets lonely on top of a pile of money
real luxury is sharing your heart with somebody

-fuck money

the darkest place in the world
where money flies and the soul dies
hoes live fake lives
snake dance and glazed eyes

-strip clubs

my life is just an empty void
filled with trauma
sex and money
because it was too hurtful to wait for you in the sun
and the stillness of the water
it hurts me more to witness magic alone
it reminds me that I have no one
who loves me as much as I love flowers
who cares like bees care for honey
watching the sunset alone used to be the saddest thing
now it's just another monday

-the wait

woke up from a nightmare
just so I can witness the sunrise
so how are you telling me
there is no light after a dark time

-4:29 am

nothing is ever left unsaid
there is not enough space in my head
to hold all these conversations
sometimes in the shower
but mostly in my room
I'm always speaking to someone
a pretend lover
an old friend
god
the stars
spirits
whoever can hear me in any dimension
so many conversations
were held in the silence of my home
and I only fear they can't come alive
sometimes it gets so lonely
I prefer to pretend someone's with me
and maybe it makes me look crazy
but crazy is still better than lonely

-lonely

my whole life
I was busy looking at other's light
I lost focus of my reflection
because I was busy looking at the glare
how bright and shiny it was
a glare that didn't belong to me
the glare wasn't mine
but it was definitely a reflection of me
so I learned to change focus
and understand that what I see in them
is exactly what lives in me

-reflection

since I was young
as far as I can remember
my heart never changed
all I ever wanted was
for everyone to be happy
genuinely and with no limits
I am very proud to have kept this heart
pure through the pain
I had all the opportunities you can imagine
to walk away from it
but I didn't
that in itself
it is my life's
greatest accomplishment

-my heart

I have written some of my best work
during some of my worst days
I am far down my spiritual journey
yet still in the beginning
I know better and have the wisdom
to know what is good or bad for me
but I just had a cigarette and a beer
some comfort food for the soul
it is a full moon in cancer
the last one of the year
I should light incense
and pray next to my candles
but the absence of his love
came back haunting me
tonight neither the moon
nor the sky could keep me
from hating me

-a stop on the road to bliss

a new journey is waiting for me
I never got to know myself outside of my sins
without the influence of the nightlife
I always melted and adapted to the city and its games
I hid in every place I could find peace and yet
god was only preparing me
something I always longed for
something I thought I was ready to receive
it was hard to admit I wasn't ready
I learned that I could feel deserving of something
and yet not be ready for it and that's ok
the bigger the blessing
the higher the level of preparation
so I am grateful for every heartbreak
friendship
loss
laughter
for every time I should've went home
instead of staying out
for the times I chose sins over abstinence
I can't say I am proud of it all
but I can sure say I didn't miss out on life

-pilgrimage

I do not wish you death
that would be too easy
but I hope you do get hit
right in front of me
somewhere in a small city
I would sit and watch you in agony
I would look in your eyes
like the day after you touched me
with the same audacity you had to smile
and say *I'm sorry*
right next to your daughter
what if she asked *sorry for what*
not one day I haven't thought
about the answer you would've given her
would I have watched you lie
or say *I touched her pussy while she was asleep*
every day you loved to have us around
watch us get ready and dress like ladies
you are the last thing I wanted to write about
you do not deserve a space in this book
but god told me this book is exactly the space
for monsters like you
because if there is one space you do not deserve to live
is in me

and just when I thought
I was looking for my father
in every man I loved
I was really looking for a mother
for an unconditional love
a nurturing love that would save me
tell me all is fine
when life gets hard
the money and the sex
could never fulfill the space
of an empty heart
of an unwanted child

-mother wound

every time I remove a layer of trauma
my bones are shaking
I am one layer closer
to being fully naked

-underneath my skin

take pride in all the love you gave freely
without expecting anything in return
pride in seeing the best in people
when they couldn't see it
loyal to a fault
broken
angry
sad
impulsive

but what I see today is a fearless woman
full of love
so full she could explode
your heart was beaten so many times
and you still wear it proudly on your sleeve
with all the scars and wounds
you have learned to stitch it and still love through it
through it all
you have died and come back to life so many times
you picked up all the pieces and made a masterpiece

-ode to my adulthood

SPIRIT

until a king butterfly lands on your soul
and then you are ready to die
do you hear your angels talking in your dreams
leading you to the rebirth of your soul
death is always near but what is death
the resurrection of your being
coming back to life
but what is life

as I come alive each rising
and die every night
my soul leaves me for a few moments
I witness it go with pain
and come back with light

-dreams

everything is dark now and I miss you
I miss your light and your magic
I know that no matter what you are present
I know you have my back
it feels selfish to ask anything from you
your work is admirable
and I don't want to take your love away
from anyone who needs it right now

please forgive me
for the times I was conceited or arrogant
for every time I gossip or hurt someone
with or without the intention of doing so
forgive me for the times I wasn't able to forgive
times I gave up
times I was inconsiderate or ungrateful
towards others and myself
please forgive me for my unborn mistakes
for all the lies and the sins

thank you for your light
for your unconditional forgiveness
thank you for loving each and every one of us
thank you for every lesson you've taught me
for pushing me to be my best self
thank you for your kindness
for giving me the heart I have
for protecting me from anything against me
but mostly thank you for peace
within and around us

-a prayer

you wake up to the whistles of angels fading
mother is an eternal source
flowers are immortal
clouds are heaven's bed
life has passed by
in a blink of an eye
you wake up from the dead

-heaven

create in the darkness of the moon
bloom in the sunlight
flow in your feelings
set your soul on fire
let everything be
and be everything
feel all of it
and be none of it

-elements

I never run out of tears
I am an infinite source of water
my fire never dies
I am an infinite source of light

so I made a vow
a vow to flourish
over and over again
I am an infinite source of life

-eternal

and we as kids
should run the world
free from pain
filled with innocence
we can trust again
even with our eyes closed
can you feel
the feeling of nothing

-freedom

the wind reminds me I'm alive
it reminds me to breathe
and that I am nowhere but here
if you listen carefully
you will hear it too

the water reminds me of my heart
overflowing with love
I am an infinite source
of compassion and kindness
I am unconditional
my love is unconditional

the sun reminds me of my inner fire
my light my passion
it reminds me of my purpose
and why I am here in the first place
the rays of light are mother talking to me
watching over me and protecting me

earth
I am her she is me
we both create and set the foundation
we work in harmony
she is precious and creative
earth inspires me to be
the creatress of my journey

the elements that surround you
are the same elements in you
and if nature has the power
to create such magic
so do you

-gaia

and if you never sin
you will never know
how to turn an empty pen
into a magic wand

-alchemist

my purpose was not meant to please those who don't choose love

-boundaries

lift your head and smile
you are loved
you are protected
you are divine

-reminder

it was a moment in time
when I was able to poke outside of my cocoon
for the very first time
I was dead and in process of rebirthing
not yet sure how things were going to unfold
I still have flashes of who I was before
but when I got to see a glimpse of life again
one with yet still so much chaos
it was enlightened with a different light
a different touch
the rain is a rare thing here
and when it does rain
we dance
we respond to things differently
so when we worry less
the worries of the world
are less than a worry

-glimpse

god is it a game for you to test me
to send me lovers covered in lies
dreams all empty inside
do you enjoy watching me fail you
and choose others over you
you took the risk and watched me
debate should I live or die
you would watch me take my own life
and send me right back where I died
are you amused by my innocence
by the hatred and the violence

-rock bottom

how can you say that stillness
does not move the world
when you know the sun is still
then watch it rise and set every day

life put me through misery so I can feel gratitude
life sent me blessings so I can give back
life put me through heartbreaks so I can love
life put me through fears so I can have faith
I was never put where I didn't belong

-where I belong

every day I look forward to another sunset
every night I look forward to another sunrise
and when there is a cloudy day
with no apparent sunset or sunrise
I hug the sky and tell it
you are not too much you are just enough

-clouds

keep a yin energy in your mind
and a yang energy in your heart
then move accordingly

-balance

this is how it feels to walk on clouds
the times in between lives where I was an angel
I could feel it under my feet palms
that same sensation when love feels calm

-angel energy

I pray in the light
and create in the dark
I was sent by the sun
and raised by the moon

who's afraid of the rain
is afraid of the truth

our biggest challenge
as conscious beings
is not knowing
we find ways to wake up each day
to find a meaning to this unknown
to control our destiny
and give it sense in some shape
form or belief

the solution to this challenge is to be
to be in each moment
in a moment of unknown

but then life loses its senses
and we simply decide that
a moment with no sense
no meaning
has less value
or no value at all
we lose sense of gratitude
that each moment is offered to us freely
and unconditionally
for no meaning
no reason
no expectation
isn't that rich enough

now once a meaning has been decided collectively on
something
then we add rules as to how it should be treated
or experienced
we have completely forgotten that we have been gifted
something that did not ask us anything in return

-it doesn't have to make sense to make sense

today I danced in the shower
I was grateful for life
grateful that kindness on my part
has played a big role in the universe
to see how my participation
in the divine orchestration
matters

-butterfly effect

today I am grieving
and giving birth
I am sad and yet
the happiest I have ever been
I am mourning and celebrating
I am in pain and healing
today I am praying
for all that has left
for all that is yet to come
and for all that I can't save
I am making peace
with divine timing

-death

the sun brightens my path
the moon has my back

-shield by god

she is deep and mysterious
scary and comforting
she can move any being
beyond what they think they are
she is the sunset's best venue
I can't always look straight into her eyes
otherwise I get caught in her riptides
I can lay in her bed of waves all day
until I drown in her love
it is not for you to understand the ocean
but to understand who you are next to her

-ode to the ocean

if every flower waited for other flowers
to bloom at the same time
out of fear of outshining each other
we wouldn't know summer
there is no sacrifice to be made
when we choose our light
but when we do not
we sacrifice our happiness
we sacrifice all the pleasures of summer
so I am thankful for flowers
who bloom unapologetically
choose you like flowers
choose themselves

-a world without summer

I float through my lessons
and all the heartbreaks
with my eyes closed
and a smile on my face
the same way I walk
through the summer breeze
my hands wide open
I welcome the divine inside me
as it flows through my fingers
and teaches me love and purity

-divine intervention

dare to be the most loving version of yourself
even if it ends
even if it's painful
there is an undeniable flow happening
do not resist the waves
for god always brings us to the shore safely
when we simply trust
that it is all part of our divine destiny

-love freely

I'm craving the feels under my fingers
this sanctuary of peace
where I can play my darkest melody
I want to lay my head on it and cry
I want to channel all my hatred into a symphony
take this escape
to a sacred place
where time is a mystery
I want to lay peacefully in that hole
let my hands sing my heart's misery

-sound healing

I think the only way to know someone
truly and authentically
is through poetry
let them write a piece of their story
of who they are or who they want to be
there is a level of vulnerability
that is undeniable
in the process of poetry
poems are our purest human form in words
the paper is your journey
the ink is your soul
make sure you write a good story

-your life is poetry

ABOUT THE AUTHOR

Sayeh Gold is Canadian born from Iranian parents. Her mother is a vipassana meditator and at the age of 21, she decided to join that journey as well. Her father was an actor, a poet, a musician, and an excellent cook. She was very inspired by both her parents, to follow her soul and creative purpose. With *Poetic Healing*, she is bringing those two passions together to help and inspire others to live authentically. *Poetic Healing* is her first publication, but Sayeh has been writing for years. She hustled her way out of her 20's as a stripper and finally found the courage to share her story with the world hoping to uplift any being coming across her words.

Manufactured by Amazon.ca
Bolton, ON

26377122R00072